# Allosaurus

## by Grace Hansen

Abdo
**DINOSAURS**
Kids

**abdopublishing.com**

Published by Abdo Kids, a division of ABDO, P.O. Box 398166, Minneapolis, Minnesota 55439.

Copyright © 2018 by Abdo Consulting Group, Inc. International copyrights reserved in all countries. No part of this book may be reproduced in any form without written permission from the publisher.

Printed in the United States of America, North Mankato, Minnesota.

052017

092017

 THIS BOOK CONTAINS RECYCLED MATERIALS

Photo Credits: Alamy, Depositphotos Enterprise, Glow Images, iStock, Science Source, Shutterstock, Thinkstock, ©Michael Overton p.21 / CC-BY-SA-2.5

Production Contributors: Teddy Borth, Jennie Forsberg, Grace Hansen

Design Contributors: Dorothy Toth, Laura Mitchell

Publisher's Cataloging in Publication Data

Names: Hansen, Grace, author.

Title: Allosaurus / by Grace Hansen.

Description: Minneapolis, Minnesota : Abdo Kids, 2018 | Series: Dinosaurs | Includes bibliographical references and index.

Identifiers: LCCN 2016962373 | ISBN 9781532100352 (lib. bdg.) | ISBN 9781532101045 (ebook) | ISBN 9781532101595 (Read-to-me ebook)

Subjects: LCSH: Allosaurus--Juvenile literature. | Dinosaurs--North America-- Juvenile literature.

Classification: DDC 567.912--dc23

LC record available at http://lccn.loc.gov/2016962373

# Table of Contents

Allosaurus . . . . . . . . . . . . . . . . . . 4

Habitat. . . . . . . . . . . . . . . . . 8

Body . . . . . . . . . . . . . . . . . . . 10

Food . . . . . . . . . . . . . . . . . . 18

Fossils . . . . . . . . . . . . . . . . . .20

More Facts . . . . . . . . . . . . . . . . .22

Glossary . . . . . . . . . . . . . . . . . .23

Index . . . . . . . . . . . . . . . . . . . .24

Abdo Kids Code. . . . . . . . . . . . .24

## Allosaurus

Allosaurus lived in the late **Jurassic period**, about 150 million years ago.

Allosaurus were **theropods**.

6

## Habitat

Allosaurus lived in plains

near rivers and lakes.

## Body

Allosaurus could weigh nearly 3,000 pounds (1,360 kg). They could grow more than 30 feet (9.1 m) long. They were 15 to 17 feet (4.6 to 5.2 m) tall.

An allosaurus had a thick,
sturdy body. It had a very
long tail.

12

13

It had two powerful legs and two short arms. Each arm ended in three long claws.

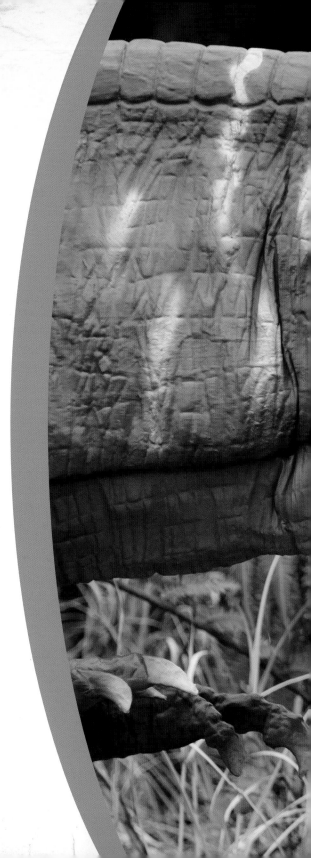

Its neck was short. Its head was large. There were two horns above its eyes.

## Food

The allosaurus was a meat

eater. It had very sharp teeth!

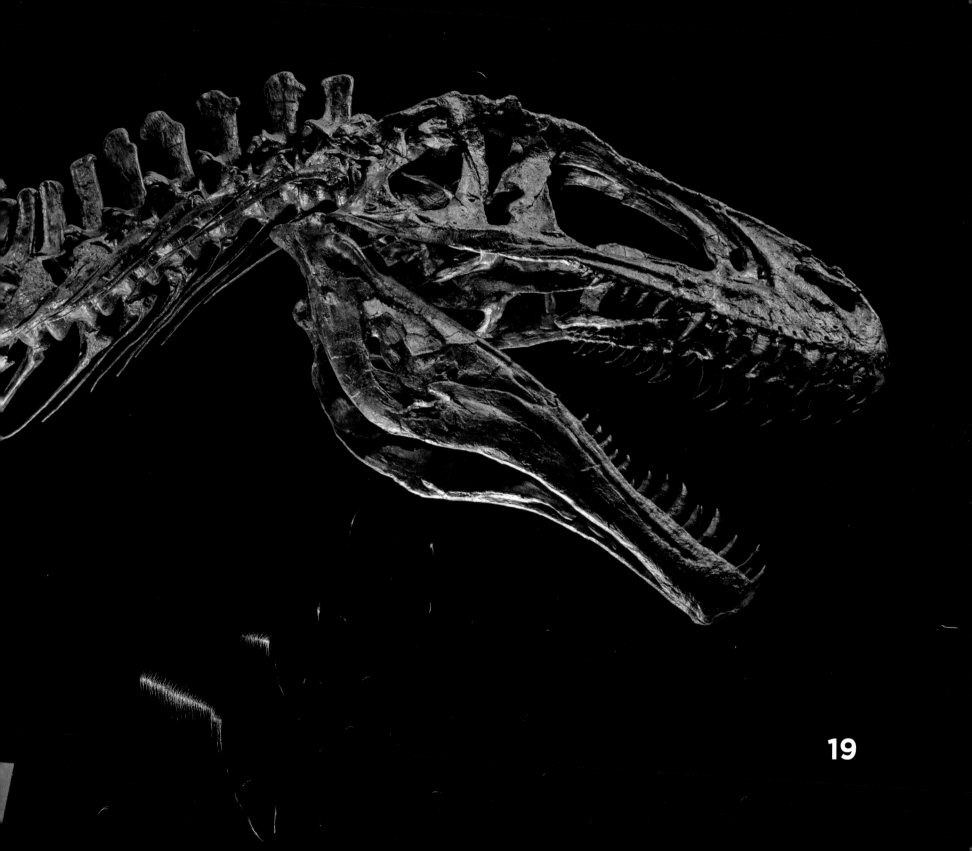

19

## Fossils

Many Allosaurus **fossils** have been found in Utah. The most fossils were uncovered in Wyoming and Colorado.

20

Wyoming

Utah

Colorado

# More Facts

- By age 15, Allosaurus had grown to their full adult size. Scientists think that Allosaurus could have lived 25 to 30 years.

- There are three main Allosaurus **species** known to scientists. The biggest difference between species is size.

- **Paleontologists** have found Allosaurus **fossils** with injuries the same shape and size as the tail spikes of Stegasaurus.

# Glossary

fossil – the remains, impression, or trace of something that lived long ago, as a skeleton, footprint, etc.

Jurassic period – named after the Jura Mountains where rocks of this age were first found, this time period saw many lush plants, large plant-eating dinosaurs, and smaller meat-eating dinosaurs.

paleontologist – a scientist who studies fossils.

species – a group of animals that look alike, share many characteristics, and can produce young together.

theropod – a meat-eating dinosaur that comes in many sizes and usually has small forelimbs.

# Index

arms 14

claw 14

Colorado 20

eyes 20

food 18

fossils 20

habitat 8

head 16

horns 16

Jurassic period 4

legs 14

neck 16

size 10

tail 12

teeth 18

theropod 6

Wyoming 20

Utah 20

## abdokids.com

Use this code to log on to abdokids.com and access crafts, games, videos and more!

Abdo Kids Code:
DAK0352